D. L. Moody
God's Salesman

D. L. Moody
God's Salesman

by
Sandy Dengler

MOODY PRESS
CHICAGO

© 1986 by
THE MOODY BIBLE INSTITUTE
OF CHICAGO

All rights reserved. No part of this book may be reproduced in any form without permission in writing from the publisher, except in the case of brief quotations embodied in critical articles or reviews.

ISBN: 0-8024-1786-8

3 5 7 9 10 8 6 4

Printed in the United States of America

*To the countless men and women
who serve, and are served by, this
shoe salesman's ministry*

Contents

CHAPTER		PAGE
	Preface	9
1.	Dwight's Speech	11
2.	Trapped	13
3.	Off to Boston	19
4.	New Job	24
5.	The Best Salesman	30
6.	Mr. Kimball	36
7.	West to Chicago	40
8.	Dwight's Town	45
9.	Old D. L.	50
10.	Mr. Farwell	55
11.	The Horse	61
12.	More Important Than Shoes	65
13.	Emma	70
14.	The War	74
15.	Schoolhouse Hospital	79
16.	God's Man	86
17.	The Big Fire	91
18.	Mr. Moody's School	97
19.	Going Home	101
	When It Happened	107

Preface

"God's servant."

That sure sounds stuffy. A no no. Even dull.

Dwight Moody was God's servant, but he was never stuffy and definitely never dull. He slammed through life joyfully, never letting setbacks hold him down for long, full of fun and enthusiasm.

God will gladly use any person devoted to Him. Here's how He used the hefty and exuberant Dwight L. Moody.

1

Dwight's Speech

"Ah-hem! Your attention, please."

Dwight Lyman Moody might be only a boy yet. Yet he was in charge of this whole town meeting. That's a big job, but no problem; Dwight was a big boy for his age. He stood up proudly at the front of the room. Just about every farmer in the area sat in the audience watching him.

Dwight began his speech. "The topic of tonight's debate is the wrongs to which Indians have been subjected."

Was Dwight ever nervous! His hands were moist, his fingers cold. His voice shook a little. He knew every person in the room (everyone always knew everyone else in these tiny Massachusetts towns). Was he making a fool of himself?

Dwight never minded acting foolish if it meant pulling off a super-great joke on someone. He was the biggest joker in Northfield. But this was different. This was supposed to be serious.

His voice faltered; his tongue stumbled. He could not remember what to say. He had practiced this speech a hundred times. Suddenly it had all trickled out of his memory like water from a basket.

"So, uh—er—the Indians went to the North Pole and got froze up stiff as steelyards." Dwight plunked down in his chair.

The farmers roared with laughter.

Why did Dwight, who wasn't even grown up, ever think he could lead a debate? He was a farm boy. He talked like a farmer. His manners were strictly country-boy. He would never be a polished speaker.

Dwight knew one thing, though; he had learned it because, just as often as he played jokes on others, other jokesters played tricks on him. He knew what to do when someone laughed at him. Dwight laughed, too.

2

Trapped

Tilting and gliding, the hawk soared low across the meadow. Its white rump patch flashed in the warm sun.

Now that's freedom.

Fifteen-year-old Dwight watched the big gray bird sweep along the meadow's edge. It skimmed the woods and floated away beyond sight on the unseen breeze. Dwight sighed. He gathered a handful of pea vines and yanked them out. He threw them on the pile and reached for another handful.

How he envied that graceful hawk riding on the wind! Dwight was tied to the dirt. He wanted to soar. Instead he pulled pea vines, leaving his footprints in the loose soil of the Connecticut River Valley. He bundled the big scratchy wads of pea vines into his arms and headed for the pigpens.

If Dwight was tied to the dirt, Patsy was

born to it. Patsy the pet pig with her four little porkers came running. They had all five been in the mud wallow recently. The caked dirt, half dry and light, half wet and dark, had turned the pink pigs brown. And the pigsty itself was nothing but dirt—rough, churned-up, beaten, dirty dirt. Pigs loved dirt. Dwight did not.

He threw the pea vines over the fence and wandered up to the house. He pushed in through the back door and checked the kitchen table for tasty morsels. He saw only a big pile of snapped green beans, and he was not hungry enough yet to eat raw string beans.

"Dwight? That you?" Ma called from the pantry.

"Yeah, Ma."

"Got the pea patch cleared?"

"Yeah, Ma."

"Good. Stay away from that pudding on the stove."

"Yeah, Ma." Dwight wagged his head. His mother was out of sight in the pantry with her back turned. How could she possibly know that his nose had just told him about the pudding?

He peeked carefully into the cookie jar. He was pretty good at opening the jar without letting the lid clink. Two forlorn oatmeal cookies lay among crumbs in the bottom. No use letting them pine away. He rescued them and gently sat the lid back on the jar.

"Dwight Moody, you're harder to fill than a freight wagon! And you hold more, too. When are you gonna quit growing?" Ma stood there with one little wisp of hair sticking to her sweaty brow. Dwight could tell when she pretended to be angry and when she really was. She was pretending.

She stood in front of him and measured his height with her hand. "I do believe you'll be the biggest boy in your class again this year."

Dwight licked his lips. "Uh, Ma, I'm not really planning to go back to school this fall. I read and write good enough. I was thinking more of going off and getting a job somewheres."

She marched to the table and began scooping green beans into the big stew pot. "Nonsense, boy. You may be the biggest fifteen-year-old around, but that's all you are. You ought to finish school. You were never apprenticed to a trade. All you know is farming. You're a part of the soil, and the soil's part of you."

"Yeah, Ma." The soil was part of him, all right. Tied to the dirt. He took his cookies outside to munch on.

Away off beyond the river on the west side

of the valley, a train whistled. Trains stayed to the tracks; in that sense they were bound to the land. But they went to far places beyond this valley. They could go clear down to Philadelphia if they had a mind to. Travel. Freedom.

Here came Dwight's older brother George driving the plow team around the corner of the barn. All steamy in the cold autumn air, the huge horses dragged a dead oak tree behind them.

The tree fell last year down by the creek, uprooted in a wind storm. The oak had once been tied to the soil, firm and solid. Now all it was was firewood.

Firewood? Next thing you know, George would be expecting Dwight to help cut up that oak into stovewood. Dead, aged oak is hard as iron. It would take them forever to saw up that monster. Dwight quietly started off in the opposite direction.

"Dwight! Hey, D. L.! Don't you go slithering off!" George yelled. "Fetch the crosscut saw."

Dwight was in for it now. He hadn't got away fast enough. Wearily he hauled the big floppy crosscut saw out of the shed. By the time he reached that enormous oak log, George had unhitched the horses.

"Y'know, George, I see an easy way to handle this job. First let's—"

"Only easy way is for you to handle your share of the work. You aren't gonna sweet-talk me into getting out of it, either. Take your end."

The saw whipped gracefully as George swung it around and set its ragged teeth down on that dark, stony log. George drew back on the handle at his end. With a heavy sigh Dwight pulled back on the handle at his end. Back and forth, back and forth they pulled. A tiny cut began to show. This would take forever.

"George? I'm thinking of leaving home. Get a real job."

"You got a real job right here. Quit riding the saw."

"Ain't riding the saw. Hit's you pushing down, not me. You know—where you work and make money. Not farming."

"Make money? We grow all our food, except sugar and tea. We cut wood for heat. We build whatever houses we need. Now you want to go make money so's you can buy food and warmth and maybe a house, right?"

"With money you can go where you want and do what you want. Travel. Be free. Not stuck in the dirt like some tree, until you fall over. Ain't you ever felt pinned down? Stuck? Trapped?"

"Nope. Feel right to home here. I'm a farmer, and so are you."

"Don't plan to stay a farmer."

"You're talking nonsense, boy. Quit riding the saw, I said."

"Ain't!" It was no use talking to George—or Ma either. They were born-and-bred farm people. They just didn't understand. Ah, but Uncle Samuel, Ma's brother, was coming up from the city over Thanksgiving. He was a city man. He'd understand. Maybe Uncle Samuel would even take Dwight back to Boston with him!

Maybe.

Dwight would do anything, just about anything, to go somewhere else and do something else besides this.

Suddenly Dwight could hardly wait till Thanksgiving. "George, quit riding the saw!"

3

Off to Boston

Spring. The ground squooshed beneath Dwight's boots, all spongy from the cold spring rain. Birds were at their busiest. The last of the geese were headed north; a scraggly skein of the noisy travelers made a ragged V above the river. Maybe it was the geese that made Dwight so restless. No. It was more than that.

He was more than halfway to the Northfield railroad station, bag in hand, when he met his brother Ed coming up the hill toward him. Now he was going to have to explain to Ed this strange yearning for freedom. And he could not explain it to himself.

But Ed did all the talking. "Wait a while. Think about it. Don't leave home." He argued and pleaded for fifteen minutes. Dwight kept listening for the train; he must not miss his train.

Suddenly Ed grew quiet. "You ain't even listening to me, little brother." He dug into his pocket. He grabbed Dwight's hand and shook it, the way grown men do. "God bless you!" he said. His own hands fell away. And Ed was gone, on up the road.

Dwight opened his hand carefully; Ed had stuffed something into it. Something? *Five dollars!* Why, five dollars would keep Dwight going a long time in Boston!

Within minutes, Dwight was sitting on that train, headed for the city. He had money, and he was on his way, away from farming—away from the dirt. Nothing would stop him now.

Boston! Now here was a real city! Why, you could just about see all the money! It didn't flap in the breeze like the flags flying here and there. It didn't come sifting down out of the sky into your pocket. But you could—well, you could *see* it.

Dwight could sense the wealth the minute he got off the train at North Station. He asked the ticket agent for directions to Court Street, and even the humble ticket agent wore an expensive silk tie. It sounded as if Court Street was about as far from the train station as Ma's cow pasture was from the church back home. Home. And now Dwight was on his way south along Boston's scrambled streets,

Off to Boston

ready to seek his fortune.

The man and the occasional ladies Dwight saw all wore fancy city clothes—expensive clothes and hardly any homespun. They strolled along looking oh so casual and sophisticated. They talked together quietly, politely. Shiny little buggies and handsome carriages crowded each other in the narrow streets.

Farm horses are big, bulky, and coarse. They can work hard to earn their keep. Farmers didn't have much use for light horses that couldn't do heavy hauling. These city horses, though, were nearly all light cart horses, with slim legs and long, thin necks. Only wealthy people owned sleek horses that could not work hard. And the buildings! Any of the big buildings here in Boston would be worth the whole town of Northfield.

The ticket agent had told Dwight that Court Street was, at most, half a mile from North Station. It seemed like five miles, perhaps because Dwight kept getting lost. He walked down Stanford Street. The sun was in his face, so he was obviously going in the right direction—south. His carpetbag was getting pretty heavy.

Now he was on Derne Street. No one had said anything about a Derne Street. He asked directions again of a cab driver. He turned left as instructed and headed east. His bag weighed a ton, and his stiffly starched collar was rubbing an open sore on his neck.

He found himself on Somerset and asked directions again. His feet hurt from walking on the rough cobblestones. Boston was losing a bit of its glamour.

And now he was standing in front of the absolutely magnificent City Hall. This was School Street. He was not supposed to be on a School Street. He asked directions and walked north, the sun at his back. His collar chafed. His bag dragged at his arm.

Court Street at last! Dwight had only to find Holton's Shoe Store, and he would be in his Uncle Samuel's welcoming arms. Finally he found the place. He was so glad, he almost forgot his aching feet and the sore on his neck and his painful arms. He stepped from sunshine into gloom. He put down his bag just inside the door.

What a dull store! Back in Northfield you bought shoes in the general store. Besides shoes, general stores had a million delightful things—candy in big glass jars, pocket knives in a display case, a couple of toys, some lovely books. This shoe store displayed shoe boxes. That was all. Rows and rows and rows of shoe boxes. Apparently customers sat in chairs in the middle of the room as they tried on shoes.

Dwight waited a moment until his eyes adjusted to the gloomy shade. There was Uncle Samuel at a counter in the back, tying string around some lady's shoe box. He had a sort of stuck-on smile on his face.

The sore on Dwight's neck hurt. His feet hurt. He was tired. But there was Uncle Samuel; soon everything would be just fine. Dwight dismissed what Uncle Samuel had said last Thanksgiving. Back then, Uncle Samuel said he didn't want Dwight in his store at all. But that was months ago. Surely Uncle Samuel had softened since then. Dwight walked across the room.

He grinned as wide as Kansas and twice as deep. "Howdy, Uncle Samuel!"

Uncle Samuel stared at him. Then he glared at him. No grin. No smile—not even a stuck-on one. The sour look on his face spoke plainly: Uncle Samuel thought Dwight ought to be home in Northfield.

Suddenly Boston was a very cold and unfriendly place.

4

New Job

Dwight was hungry. A boy his size—extra large—eats a lot. Back home in Northfield there would be plenty of good food on the table. Dwight tried not to think about fresh warm cornbread, rich bean soup, fried chicken, or golden sweet potatoes all glistening with sugar and butter.

He reached deep into his pocket. That five dollars Ed had given him was nearly gone already. And yet Dwight had been in Boston less than a week. In a big city like this money just melted away!

Here was Dwight's favorite bakery. He stepped inside. The bakery was much brighter than Uncle Samuel's shoe store; it had bigger windows and more of them. And the smells? Um-um-um! Dwight studied the bread and cookies and rolls a long time.

He pointed. "One of those, please." It was

not his favorite kind of roll, but it was the biggest roll for the price. Dwight paid his penny and walked out into Copley Square.

Dwight loved this part of Boston. Even on a cloudy day like today the buildings fairly gleamed. All the people walking to and fro across the square were elegant people who dressed well. This was Dwight's kind of city. A person could go far here.

Some persons could. It did not seem that Dwight was getting anywhere. You would think in a town this big someone would be ready to hire a strong, eager young man. No. After a whole week of job hunting, Dwight was still without work.

He sighed. He wished Uncle Samuel liked him better. He wished he could find a job. He wished lots of things that just weren't so. That sore on his neck was now a full-blown boil, a fire-hot blister of constant pain. Every time he turned his head his collar mashed it, twisted it, made it stab into him.

He walked slowly back toward home. Home? This wasn't home. He was living with his mother's other brother, Lemuel Holton. Uncle Lemuel's house was not a bit like home. It was dark. Quiet. There were never any good cooking smells.

Dwight pushed in through the door of Uncle Lemuel's house.

"That you, Dwight?" Uncle Lemuel called from somewhere.

"Yes, sir." Dwight wandered down the dark, cool hall. He wondered if the house stayed this clammy all summer. Here was Uncle Lemuel in the sitting room.

"Well, lad, found a job worthy of you?"

"Not yet. Thinking of walking down to New York. Lotsa work there."

Uncle Lemuel studied him a moment. "Sit down, boy."

Dwight sat. Without moving his head.

"You know how far away New York is?"

"Bout a hundred miles, I suppose."

"Closer two hundred. Dwight, lad, you got enough pride, but sometimes a man needs modesty more than pride. Humility. Like for instance to go back and tell your uncle you'd be pleased to learn the shoe business from him."

"He knows I'm in Boston. If he wanted me he'd say so." His boil ached. His stomach growled; the bakery roll hadn't been enough. "Besides, what if he says no?"

"You just have to take that chance."

"Supposing I don't want to?"

"Then it's back to the farm."

The farm. Dirt. Dirt and hard work and no pay.

Dwight lurched to his feet. "Be back in a

couple hours." He walked down the long, dark, lonely hallway. He stepped out into dull and overcast daylight. Back to the farm? He'd crawl to New York first.

He took his time walking over to Court Street. He paused a few minutes on Boston Common. The murky waters of the Charles River lapped at the shore along the common's west side. He had heard that someone planned to fill in the river basin along here— make more land for the city to grow upon. Somehow the common would not be quite the same if it lost its river bank.

In his mind he compared this Charles River with his Connecticut River back home. They were not the least alike. The river back home—*his* river—flowed solidly and honestly. It rushed high and turbid in spring, dark and quiet in autumn.

The Charles slopped listlessly, rising and falling with the tide. The ocean mixed salt water into its stream, making the river a cloudy, unappetizing gray. Dwight left the slack river behind and walked on east to Court Street.

On a sunny day, Holton's Shoe Store was a gloomy place. Today with the overcast it felt gloomier than ever inside. He sat in a chair to wait; his uncle was serving two ladies. Dwight tried to find a way to keep his collar off his boil. There didn't seem to be any. The two customers left with their shoe boxes.

Dwight stood up. "Uncle Samuel, I'd like to talk to you."

"Thought you would." The scowl on Uncle Samuel's face brightened to a smile. "You have to wait. Here comes a customer." The smile fled. He studied Dwight closely. "Do you want to wait?"

"Yes, sir." Dwight was getting pretty good at waiting. He was going to have to get good at swallowing pride, too. That would be a lot harder than waiting.

Finally the customer left. Dwight followed Uncle Samuel into the back room.

Uncle Samuel looked like the Greek god of thunder standing there, his face dark as a storm cloud. "I allow as how I have some obligation to help your ma, my poor brave sister. So I'll take you on as a stock boy."

Dwight was all set to whoop joyfully, but Uncle Samuel grabbed his coat lapel and jerked it, bringing Dwight up nose to nose with him. The painful boil stabbed.

"Listen sharp, boy. My store here is a proper establishment, and, frankly, I don't even want you around. You're too wild and unpredictable. The tricks you play, and the way you talk. If you work here you'll stay at a boardinghouse of *my* choosing. You'll behave

New Job

yourself, stay off the street at night, and go to church and Sunday school both—every week!"

Uncle Samuel went on with more rules. Dwight's boil hurt so badly he couldn't even hear. But it didn't matter. He'd do just about anything to stay here in the city. Even go to church.

Church! Hmph. Sunday school. Double hmph. What had God ever done for Dwight? Or for Dwight's ma and brothers, for that matter? Dwight didn't even think about God. But he would do anything his uncle wanted. He would not go back to the farm. To the dirt.

He would even go to church.

5

The Best Salesman

"And so I cut a long slit in the seat of his leather stool, see? And put a basin of water underneath it." Dwight slowed his walk a bit. John, the young man with him, had short legs; the fellow was huffing and puffing to keep up.

Dwight continued. "It worked! The cobbler sits down on his stool and sags down right into the cold water." John was giggling already. "But that ain't the funniest part. The funniest part is, he sat down that way *three times* before he kicked his stool over to see what was getting him so wet!"

John laughed. "And what'd he do to you?"

"Chased me with a leather knife. I ran out of the store till he cooled off some. I lost a sale, too, 'cause I was waiting on a customer when he come after me."

John was roaring. "Serves you right!" The

laugh quieted. "I know how important sales are to you."

Dwight bobbed his head. "Y'know, John, I'm gonna earn myself a hundred thousand dollars. That's my goal. Hundred thousand. Be a merchant. Own my own store. Why already I'm the best salesman in my uncle's store. I can do it."

"Don't doubt it. Here we are; the courthouse."

A mob of men had gathered at the foot of the courthouse steps. Dwight was simply one of many. He recognized a lot of them, too. These were the people who came to the abolitionist meetings over in Faneuil Hall.

When Dwight first came to Boston he had never even heard the word *abolition*. Now here he was in the thick of it. He knew as much about it as he needed to know: abolition meant ending slavery. Dwight could not imagine that any human being had the right to own another human being. The stirring speakers at the meetings had convinced him to fight for an end to slavery.

A large man stepped out of the crowd onto the steps. "Bring Anthony Burns out!" he shouted at the courthouse door. "We know you're holding him."

Where did the soldiers come from? Young men in militia uniforms had just appeared at the top of the steps. They carried rifles. Dwight wasn't too worried yet. Surely nobody was going to shoot anybody over an escaped slave.

"What's going on here?" A well-dressed older gentleman stepped in beside Dwight.

John answered. "An escaped slave named Burns was captured, and his owners want him back. We want him free."

The man glared at John. "I can't see that it's any of your business. An owner should be able to retrieve his property without a mob of ruffians snarling at him."

John smirked. "No property list should have people on it."

Dwight's attention snapped to the courthouse steps. The soldiers and the large fellow were shouting at each other.

"Here's the planks!" called someone from the rear. "Break the door down!" From man to man, they were passing around huge, heavy wooden boards—battering rams.

This was getting serious—and exciting! Was Dwight going to stand here and watch? Or was he going to be part of the action? All his life he had taken part in the action. In fact, he often started the action. He didn't even think about it. He was ready to help bash in that door!

The Best Salesman

Bla-blam! Two soldiers' guns went off, almost as one.

Murky gray gunsmoke drifted down the courthouse steps.

"Disperse!" cried a young soldier. All but two rifles were leveled on the crowd now. Should they fire they could not help but hit people. The soldiers with the two spent rifles were reloading quickly, expertly.

The angry, shouting mob became an upset, mumbling mob. The mass moved back a bit, crowding against John and Dwight.

John's mouth was a thin, tight line. "We could lose a couple lives here and still not reach Burns. Methinks 'tis time to regroup."

"What?" Dwight used plain words. Country words. He had trouble following fancy city speech.

"Retreat."

"That I understand." Dwight's breastbone tingled; his hands shook a little. He was excited! He wanted to do something, to help someone, to strike a blow for freedom! But he was just a country boy. He didn't know what to do. Apparently, neither did anyone else. The crowd broke up and, by degrees, melted away. The noble cause, which had begun so boldly, simply fizzled out.

The two boys walked in silence. All around

them, Boston bustled about on its business, as if it did not matter that Anthony Burns was not free.

"John? You suppose my whole life's gonna go like that?"

"Like what? Almost ripping the courthouse apart? Almost getting shot at?"

"Just that: almost. We didn't bash the door down; just almost. We didn't really get shot at. We almost rescued him. But we didn't. And nobody else cares but a couple of us; and we don't care enough to put our lives on the line. Is my life gonna just be one almost after another? Is there anything people care so much about that it doesn't just trickle away, like today did?"

John shrugged. "God maybe, if there is one. Some people will die for their religion. Not me. I don't even go to church."

"I do; Uncle Samuel said I had to if I want to work for him. He even picked the church. Mount Vernon Church."

"Edward Kirk is the preacher there, right? I hear he's real fire-and-brimstone—and very well-spoken."

Dwight half smiled. "Uncle Samuel said I had to go. He didn't say what I had to do when I got there. So I pick a seat way up in the gallery and take a nap."

John laughed. "Growing boy like you needs his rest."

"Don't sleep through Sunday school, though. The teacher's a Mr. Kimball. Ed Kimball. Older fellow, gray-haired, kinda skinny. But does he ever know his Bible! Worth listening to."

"Really!" John was grinning. "I never would have picked you to be a Bible thumper. You seem to love life too much. You like to tease; play tricks; have fun. Not exactly what I'd call pious."

Play tricks. Yep! Dwight could sure play tricks, all right. Tricks weren't much to boast about. The tricks didn't ever help him toward his goal of making a hundred thousand dollars. In fact, they cost him sales now and then. And they might be fun, but they couldn't be called "important."

What *was* important? The unfortunate slave Anthony Burns? Anthony Burns's freedom? Dwight's? God was no doubt important, but to what degree?

Making money. That was important! Dwight would concentrate on that first. He would become the best salesman in Boston. Then he would become the best salesman in the whole country.

The world would hear about Dwight Moody, salesman!

6

Mr. Kimball

Ah, spring. Back home on the farm, everyone would be busy now. This was the season when cows bore their calves and sheep their lambs. Patsy the sow would have another litter of squirmy little porkers. Ed would be turning over the soil in Ma's vegetable garden, although the big fields were still too wet to plow.

What was Dwight doing in this damp spring weather? The same thing he had been doing now for two years. Selling shoes. Cleaning up the back room. Unpacking boxes. Farmers were bound to the seasons. Selling shoes had very little to do with seasons. You came to work every day, did about the same thing day in and day out, then went home tired at night.

Dwight missed the farm. But he loved working in the city. He loved the bustle. He

Mr. Kimball 37

loved the grace and elegance of city people with their city ways. He could not imagine ever going back to the farm. Besides, he was making far more money as a shoe salesman and stock boy than he could ever make as a farmhand.

This dank and foggy day he was in the dreary back room of the shoe store, doing one of his ordinary jobs. He was wrapping shoe boxes in brown paper.

"Hey, D. L.? Someone to see you," a clerk called. And now here was a gray-haired fellow standing in the doorway.

In the room at Mt. Vernon Church where Dwight's Sunday school class met, Mr. Kimball the teacher looked very impressive. Here in the back room of Holton Shoe Store, he appeared out of place. He must have felt out of place, too; he seemed just plain nervous.

"Dwight." He invented a smile.

"Mr. Kimball. Uh, anything wrong?"

"No. Nothing wrong."

Dwight grinned. "Then how about letting me sell you a good pair of boots?" Dwight was ready to sell shoes to anyone.

"Uh, no. Not today. I want to sell *you* something."

"Sell me what?" Dwight was supposed to be the salesman.

"Well, not sell exactly. *Give* you something.

If you'll take it."

Now Dwight really was confused.

"Dwight," said Mr. Kimball, "God loves you. His Son, Jesus Christ, died for you. I want to know if you believe that. I want to know before another Sunday goes by."

Something was very out of place here. Church and Sunday school were where you talk about Jesus. This was just a stock room. It smelled like new shoes and cut leather. It was a place of business, not of God.

And yet, Mr. Kimball made talking about Jesus here seem very natural. Dwight had really never given the question any thought before. When you think about Jesus in church on Sunday, it's not the same thing as thinking or talking about Him the other six days of the week.

"Well, uh—nobody's ever really come out and asked me that before. But now that I think about it, yes. Sure! Sure I believe Jesus died for my sins."

Dwight didn't have to think about it any longer. If Jesus paid for his sins on Sunday, it figures they were paid for the rest of the week as well. The idea of being safe in Jesus made Dwight feel bouncy and happy inside.

The feeling grew. Dwight just bubbled! "Yes, sir, Mr. Kimball! And you know what? From now on I'm going to try hard to live like

I believe it! Watch and see!"

When Dwight left work and started home that evening, that special feeling still bubbled inside him. The fog had lifted; bright spring sun—the very freshest kind of sun—washed across the whole city. It made Boston Common a cheery green. It even made the Charles River sparkle, and that's doing something.

Birds were setting up their spring housekeeping all over the green—indeed, all over town. They sang here, and they sang there. Dwight had never really noticed them before; suddenly he loved to hear their sweet songs.

Dwight Moody, soon to be the world's greatest salesman, had found Jesus. How happy could a fellow be? Now he had everything!

7

West to Chicago

What a tattered old horse. She must have been lovely once, before a lifetime of hard work wrecked her. Black, bald scars here and there made her ragged gray coat look all the worse. She ought to be chunky, like the fine draft horses back on the Moody farm. But the fat muscles were gone from her ribs and hips. Even her long horse face hung in its bridle all bony and scuffed.

A farm boy knows just where to scratch. Dwight rubbed behind her ears and between her front legs. When he scratched her throat where it met her chin, she thrust out her nose and closed her eyes.

"So, old girl. You're hauling a dirt wagon. Quite a mess they're making, ain't it?" Dwight stood on the edge of Boston Common, watching men and horses work together.

They were starting to fill in the Charles

River basin along the shore here. When the project was complete, people said, new-made land would extend clear down to Roxbury neck. Boston city, bounded on three sides by water, needed more land to grow on.

"I'm surprised they're actually doing it," he told the horse. "The fuddy-duddies in this town don't never like an idea unless it's two hundred years old. Stuffy old town, Boston." Dwight dug into his pocket for some treat. Here was his apple from lunch. He took a couple of bites and fed the core to the horse.

"You know—" He chucked the mare under the chin. "Right after I became a Christian I asked to be a member of the church. Only natural, right? And the deacons turned me down. Said I didn't know enough about the faith. I knew Jesus died for my sins. That oughta be enough, don'tcha think?"

The old horse slobbered sweet foam, crunching her apple.

"And I been going to Wednesday night prayer meeting, too, without my uncle telling me to. 'Cause I *want* to. And I speak up now and then and testify. But my uncle says some folks—proper folks—don't like me to. Proper, hah! Stuffy old town."

The mare swallowed with a gentle *glunk* and shoved her face up against him, begging for more.

"And then there's my uncle." Dwight rubbed her velvet nose. "Just as stuffy as they come. I rearranged his shoe store so's he'd sell more shoes, and he made me change it back. 'That's not how it's done in Boston!' he says. Y'know, old horse? I'm just about fed up with stuffy old Boston."

He gave the horse's neck a final pat and walked off toward home. In the distance a train whistle hooted. It sounded like the trains that rolled up and down his Connecticut River Valley. It sounded like freedom.

Boston was a nice enough place, but Dwight wasn't really free here. He got lots of new ideas, all the time. He wanted some place where he would be free to try out his ideas. Maybe they'd work, maybe they wouldn't. But at least he should be able to try.

Dwight packed his clothes—what few he owned. He said good-bye to his uncles. At South Station he stepped aboard a train, and he was on his way west.

He passed up Columbus and Cleveland. He rode straight through Detroit. Chicago would be Dwight Moody's city! He had heard that Chicago was young and bold—that Chicago thrived on new ideas—that "proper" was not the most important thing a person had to be in Chicago.

West to Chicago

In the dark of night, September 13, 1856, Dwight Moody stepped onto the train platform in Chicago. He was alone.

He had proved himself a good shoe salesman back in Boston; but this was a new and different city. He was still in his teens; that's awfully young to be alone.

Dwight didn't know a solitary soul in the city. He had no idea which streets went where. He knew the town was big—the vast railroad freight yards his train had passed told him that. But where was the place for Dwight Moody, shoe salesman? For that matter, where ought Dwight spend the rest of this first night?

Ah, but farm boys with lots of good ideas don't stay lost and alone for very long. Two Christian ladies whom he had met on the train helped him find lodging. And he had Jesus. He sought out a prayer meeting a couple days later. The people there adopted him like a brother.

Before a week went by, Dwight had made new friends from among the people at the prayer meeting. He found a good church to worship in. And within two weeks he had a job—shoe salesman in Wiswell's Shoe Store.

Right from the first, he made thirty dollars a week, a marvelous amount of money for a country boy. If this kept up, he would soon earn his hundred thousand dollars.

Best of all, when Dwight wanted to try out some new idea, nobody told him "that just isn't *done* in Chicago!" Jesus, fortune, and freedom—everything Dwight wanted most was right here in Chicago.

Dwight L. Moody, the world's greatest shoe salesman, at last was on his way.

8

Dwight's Town

"Boston is a whole nuther world, lemme tellya!" Dwight jumped a rain puddle. His three friends, young men as burly as he, jumped it, too. "People so stiff and straight-laced. One of my favorite jokes—"

"You didn't play jokes in *Boston!*" Pete giggled.

"Didn't I! One of my favorites was, you fall in beside some fellow who's just walking down the street minding his own business. See? Stare straight at him without blinking, and just walk along with him. Don't say nothing. Pretty soon he's walking faster. And acting more uncomfortable. You just keep a-staring. Then he breaks into a run, and so you break into a run, too."

Dwight didn't get to finish describing his joke because his friends were howling with laughter.

"I'm not so sure it'd work here in Chicago." Pete was laughing. "People here don't seem to mind if you act goofy."

"Right!" Dwight agreed. "And you know? I think that's one of the things I like best about Chicago. People act themselves. Some farmer comes in for boots and he has big feet, he admits it. None of this nonsense about the boots being too small."

"You doing all right at Wiswell's Shoe Store then, hey?" asked Mike.

"I guess all right! I been promoted. Mr. Wiswell added a jobbing department and put me in charge." Dwight waved a hand toward the big church beside them. "Here we are."

Pete stopped inside the church's huge double doors. He looked down the long, long aisle. "Sure a big place, D. L. You certain they don't mind if we come in?"

"That's another thing I like about Chicago." Boldly, Dwight led the way right down that long aisle to the very front pews. "Now when I first got here I felt kinda lost—no family, no friends, no church—just like you fellows must feel."

"Sure do," Pete cut in. A thin film of homesickness softened his voice.

"Right. So I rented these pews down front, see? Now you and I and any other fellers who feel a little lost all have a church to come to

Dwight's Town

whenever we want. I could never do that in Boston. The deacons would turn purple, and my uncle would scold me from dawn to Tuesday. Here, all they say is, 'Right this way, gentlemen.' "

"Never heard of renting a seat for yourself in a church," Mike mumbled. "Don't do that back home."

Dwight smiled gently. "You ain't home no more."

But Dwight was home, all right. Chicago was his town! Here at last he felt free. When he wanted to bring a bunch of ordinary guys dressed in ordinary clothes into the church, no one scowled. When he stood up to give a testimony at prayer meetings, people listened. No one complained that he talked too much.

He was still a farm boy, rough-cut and unpolished. But so were all these Illinois farmers who flocked into the city. Indeed, Chicago was more a huge farm town than a proper city. Farmers brought their cattle and wheat and hogs to be sold, for Chicago had more miles of railroad than any other city in the world. Its stockyards were the nation's biggest.

And Dwight Moody, born and bred a farmer, fit right in. True, Chicago was not all excitement and freedom. The city had her sad places. The corner of Chicago Avenue and Wells Street was one of them. Garbage and sewage mixed with street mud to make the whole place stink. Run-down tenement houses held more people than they had been built to hold—people with neither hope nor money. Dirty children in ragged clothes—children by the score—sat on the unswept steps or played in the gutters.

Dwight was passing that very corner one day when a sign above a tenement door caught his eye:

MISSION

Dwight marched right inside.

The man who greeted him in the hallway looked just as tired and run-down as the building looked. "Yes?"

"Dwight L. Moody." Dwight put on his shoe-selling smile. "Friends here usually just call me D. L. I saw your sign out front. You hold services on Sundays?"

"Sunday school."

"Ah! I'm a great believer in Sunday school. A Sunday school teacher first introduced me to Jesus Christ. Tell you what! I have a little free time on Sundays. I'll come down here and teach a class for you."

"Don't need teachers. Got more teachers

than kids. A dozen kids; sixteen at the outside."

Dwight frowned. "But there's plenty of kids right on your doorstep there!"

"Right. But they don't come in. Make you a deal. You bring them in, and you can teach the class."

Dwight changed his shoe-selling smile into an aha-a-challenge grin. "It's a deal."

He left the building and simply stood on the front stoop a couple minutes, watching the children on Wells Street. Unwashed, badly fed, poorly cared for—and yet they were children just like any other children. And they needed Jesus just as much as any fancy child did.

It would take a fine piece of salesmanship indeed to sell these tattered urchins on coming to Sunday school.

And Dwight L. Moody, super-duper salesman, was just the man to do it.

9
Old D. L.

She sat on the tenement steps, scrawny and ill-fed. With tangles in her hair and dirt on her face, she did not look a bit like a Sunday school pupil. She looked very much like she needed Sunday school—and Jesus.

Dwight stopped by the steps. He sat down on his heels so he could look right across into her sad eyes. "Hi. Folks call me D. L., and I sell shoes. I also help out at Sunday school. How about coming to Sunday school this afternoon?"

She shook her head. "I don't have a nice dress."

"Good!" He grinned. "Nobody fancy at this Sunday school. If you dressed up too fancy you might feel out of place. But that dress you're wearing now will fit right in."

She looked down at her lap. "I don't know—"

Old D. L.

"You'll love it! Lots of stories about lions and donkeys and men who do great things and men who make mistakes—we might even let you in on the secret of how to be happy."

"I guess—"

Dwight hopped to his feet. "Great! Three o'clock at the mission on Wells Street. Just a short time from now."

He continued on up the street. Half a block from the tenement he glanced over his shoulder. She was coming down off the steps, running to catch up to him.

Here were half a dozen scruffy little boys. Dwight passed around six small pieces of licorice candy as he told them about the Sunday school. Four of them had been to Sunday school before. All six agreed to join him now.

Next Dwight came upon a game of catch. "Hey, boys! Playing catch with that old ball ain't much fun. Come along to Sunday school and *really* enjoy yourselves!" Four ex-ball players fell in behind. He must walk faster now; children that age get bored quickly. His rag-tag army was growing rapidly.

Two girls joined the parade here, and three others there. The children laughed. They jostled and shoved each other off the curb into the muddy, smelly gutters.

Like a mighty general, D. L. Moody led his wild and noisy soldiers off to Sunday school.

Tomorrow a few of these children—the lucky ones—would go to school. A few would have nothing to do but hang around on the rickety steps of home. Most of them, though, would go to work. They would put in very long hours for very low pay; after all, everyone knew a child should not earn as much as a grown-up, not even if he worked every bit as hard.

The gaggle of children broke up into their various classes. The whole building grew slightly quieter—only slightly. Dwight felt a tap on his arm and turned.

Mr. Stillson stood there grinning. "Hello, D. L.! How's today?"

"Good! Good. How's your day?" Dwight headed for the door.

Mr. Stillson fell in beside him. "Fine. Got a freighter coming in from Cleveland. Want to go along?"

Dwight stepped outside into the damp autumn breeze. "Sure. I brought the children in; so now my work here is finished for the day. How about stopping at those taverns along the Sands, too?"

"Yes. I was thinking we might." Mr. Stillson smiled. "Some pretty rough characters up there. I appreciate having a big, burly farm boy like you along."

Dwight laughed. Then his grin faded. "Did

Old D. L.

you notice who came to Sunday school today? And who didn't?"

"Not especially. Seemed as wild a bunch as ever. Lot of girls. More girls than usual maybe."

"We've lost a lot of the boys—boys who need the message of God's love most of all. Red Eye, Jackie Candles, others like them. I've been thinking of starting up my own Sunday school. Want to join in with me?"

"Where?" Very carefully, Mr. Stillson walked around a dead cat in the gutter. They crossed the street and headed for the lakefront docks.

"Got a vacant saloon lined up, but it's pretty small. I have my eye on North Market Hall. It would take a lot of kids to fill that place!"

"If anyone could pull the children in, it's you. And North Market Hall is certainly right in the middle of the poor district. City owns it, right?"

"Right."

They stopped short as a big freight wagon rumbled past. Mr. Stillson stepped out into the muddy street. "Hold dances there on Saturday night, don't they?"

"Just about every week, yes."

"So after the dances on Saturday night, you turn it into a church on Sunday. Think people will mind that?"

"The people I want to reach won't."

The gentle autumn breeze among those tightly-packed houses became a cold and clammy wind here on the lakeshore. Dwight turned up his collar and hunched his shoulders.

The freighter Mr. Stillson had mentioned was just docking. Children were Dwight's ministry. Ships' hands and longshoremen were Mr. Stillson's. Dwight liked being a part of it; he liked talking to these plain, hard-boiled working men.

They spoke to each sailor as he stepped off his boat. They gave each man a tract and invited him to church services.

Next they would amble over to the taverns just inland of the docks, armed with nothing more than a smile and God's good grace. They would talk to tough drinking men, all of whom were certain Jesus was a sissy.

Dwight enjoyed every bit of it. His time in Boston and his year-and-a-half spent here in Chicago had not changed his speech at all. He still sounded like a farmer. He still sounded "down home." He might not seem very polished to a fancy person, but these rough customers didn't trust fancy people. They seemed to like old D. L. well enough, though.

And old D. L. liked just about everybody.

10

Mr. Farwell

Bonk-itty conk donk donk! A whisky bottle went bouncing across the floor. With a whoop, the boy called Smikes swatted it again with his broom. It bounded, clunking, into the corner where the rest of the trash was being swept.

At the front of the room, the boy Dwight knew only as Greenhorn called, "Hey, Indian! Help me put up the Sunday school class banners."

In the middle, two very small boys were busy picking up the cigar butts squashed into the floor by many dancing feet.

Smikes snorted. "Folks sure make a mess when they go dancing on a Saturday night! I get a little tired of cleaning up after them on Sunday morning here."

Dwight grinned. "Sweeping up is just as much a service to Jesus as preaching is. Maybe more. You can get along without preachers. You can't get along without janitors."

Smikes cackled gleefully. He trooped off in search of more dirt to sweep.

Dwight walked down to the far and of the huge room. He started the lengthy task of setting up chairs. Each week they set up hundreds of chairs. This afternoon every chair would hold a bouncing, squirming, noisy boy or girl. Today those hundreds of children would hear the gospel of Jesus.

Here was Dwight L. Moody, who never finished grammar school, running his own Sunday school at the age of twenty-one. That couldn't be anything short of God's good grace in him. He quit wrestling chairs a moment to watch the boys—"Moody's bodyguard"—put the finishing touches to the vast North Market Hall.

"Good. You made it back." From out of nowhere, Mr. Stillson had appeared at his side. "How do you like your new job, D. L.?"

"Good morning! Fine. Splendid." Dwight forgot for a moment about Sunday schools. Now he was talking about selling shoes, his other love. "With Mr. Wiswell I sold shoes in only one store. But with Mr. Henderson, I travel all over. All over. Anywheres from Missouri to Minnesota. Over to Indiana, out to Iowa—"

Mr. Stillson laughed. "The railroads are making a fortune on you—traveling so much."

"Not a bit! When Mr. Henderson first offered me the job I had trouble saying yes. It was a fine chance to get ahead—to make that hundred thousand dollars I'm gonna earn. But Mr. Henderson expected me to stay out on the road three weekends of every month and come home only on the last one."

"You would've had to give up the Sunday school."

"That's what I told him. And he said he couldn't afford to bring me back to Chicago any oftener'n that. So I—"

Smikes paused by Dwight's elbow. "That be all, Mr. Moody?"

"Looks good! See you at three!"

"You bet! I might even make a penny or two before then." Grinning, Smikes snatched up his shoeshine box from beside the door. He trotted out in search of unshined boots.

"So I didn't know what to do," Dwight went on. "If I stopped coming every Sunday, a lot of these children would stop coming, too. And yet, the job was too good to pass up."

Mr. Stillson and Dwight walked out the door together.

Dwight continued, "I happened to talk

about my problem with Colonel Hammond one Sunday."

"Hammond. He's the superintendent of the Chicago, Burlington, and Quincy Railroad."

"That's right! And after I explained it all, he gets a funny grin on his face and digs a little piece of pink cardboard out of his pocket. 'That's a free pass, my boy,' he tells me. 'You can ride anywhere you want on the C, B, and Q. For nothing!' " Dwight spread his arms as wide as the grin on his face. "So here I am, every Sunday, selling Jesus. And traveling and selling shoes the other six days. It's glorious!"

"Glorious!" Mr. Stillson reached the corner first and stopped. His laughter faded. He looked ahead, down a narrow, dirty street. He glanced from side to side, up and down another street just as dirty. He looked behind them, and Dwight could read his heart from the look on his face.

Dwight nodded, agreeing with the thought Mr. Stillson had not put into words. "So many people lost here. Not just the children—everybody. They all need Jesus."

"Ah." Mr. Stillson brightened. "On the other hand, we are reaching *some* of the lost. That's better than nothing." He nodded slightly. "I'll see you at three, Lord willing."

"Lord willing. Oh!" Dwight raised a finger.

Mr. Farwell

"We have a guest this afternoon. John Farwell heard about our Sunday school, so I invited him to come observe."

Mr. Stillson gaped. "He's the wealthiest dry goods merchant in town!" He chuckled. "These wolves we teach should give him some pretty good observations."

Sure enough. As Sunday school began that afternoon, the very smart, very rich, very important Mr. John V. Farwell came walking in. Instantly, a hundred boys with shoeshine boxes crowded in close around him.

"Shine, Mister?" "Shine, Mister?" "Shine, Mister?"

Mr. Moody restored order. Mr. Stillson offered a particularly fervent prayer. Mr. Carter led the singing as he did each week. And then Mr. Moody invited Mr. Farwell to speak.

Dwight had an idea. He was a good salesman—even a great salesman—but when it came to running this huge, unruly Sunday school, he needed help. Mr. Farwell here was a proved leader who knew how to organize a business. And this Sunday school was God's business. Folks might call it "Moody's Sunday school," but it wasn't Dwight's at all. It belonged to Dwight's Lord.

Mr. Farwell completed his speech. He sat down as the children clapped and cheered. Clapping and cheering? In Sunday school?

The man appeared a bit uneasy.

Dwight stood up. "Wonderful!" He was clapping, too. "Isn't Mr. Farwell a fine gentleman?"

More clapping.

"He would be the perfect superintendent for this Sunday school, would he not?"

Mr. Farwell sputtered, his eyes wide with surprise.

Dwight hurried on: "This Sunday school is for all of you; to help you find life in Jesus Christ. So it stands to reason you ought to have a part in choosing its superintendent. All those in favor of electing Mr. Farwell here, who spoke so beautifully—?"

The joy of God and joy of man joined together in the rowdy crowd. They voted by clapping, cheering, and stomping.

"Yes! And those opposed?" Dwight wheeled. "Then it's unanimous! Congratulations, Superintendent Farwell!" He extended his hand to shake.

Dwight was afraid for a moment that Mr. Farwell would not be taken in by his fast sales pitch. Perhaps Dwight had pushed too hard and too far. Perhaps he should have—

The businessman stood up. Suddenly he grasped Dwight's hand. "I guess I can spot a chance to serve God when it slaps me this hard. Very well. I accept." He was laughing. "Mr. Moody, you are quite some salesman!"

11

The Horse

"So how do you like it?" Dwight rubbed the soft velvet nose of his brand new horse.

"It's beautiful!" The little dark-haired girl reached out timidly to pet its shoulder. "I just love spotted horses!"

"Ugly thing," the boy beside her mumbled. He crossed his arms and took a shuffling step backward.

"Is it a Christmas present?" she asked. "It's almost Christmas, you know."

Dwight laughed. "Nope. I bought him so I could travel around town here faster to do my visiting. Invite folks to Sunday school and to meetings and services in the evenings. How would you like to come to Sunday school this afternoon?"

She shrugged bashfully. "Guess so."

Dwight looked the sullen boy right in the eye. "And what'll it take to get you to come?"

The boy was a conniver; you could see plots hatching all over his face. "A ride on your ugly old horse there."

"It's a deal!" Dwight handed him the reins and walked over to the tenement steps. He sat down on the second step.

At first the boy didn't seem to believe it. Suddenly he grinned. He struggled mightily to get the loop of reins up over the weary old horse's head.

The horse stood patiently, its ears all floppy, as the boy jumped up and down trying to get his foot in a stirrup—got a foot in the stirrup—realized it was the wrong foot and started over—got the other foot in the stirrup—hauled himself hand-over-hand up the stirrup leathers—reached the seat—squirmed and kicked—and finally hauled himself aboard.

He dragged the horse's head around and thumped with his heels. With a sigh the horse plodded off. This was not the first little boy it had taken for a ride.

The little girl sat down beside Dwight on the steps. "I was kinda hoping that was a Christmas present from your lady friend. Something romantic. Do you have a lady friend?"

Dwight grinned at her. "Funny you should ask. Couple months ago I would've said no.

But the answer's yes now. Yes, I got me a lady friend."

"What's her name?"

"Emma. Emma Revell. She's real young—not more'n halfway through her teens. But she's pretty. So mighty pretty. And a good Christian, too. Teaches a Sunday school class."

The little girl's eyes sparkled. "That's so romantic. What does she call you? 'Sweety'? 'Honey'?"

"D. L."

Her face pinched together in a frown. "That's all? D. L.?"

At the far end of the block, the boy was twisting the horse's head around, heading it back this way again.

"That's what everyone calls me. Ain't that enough?"

"Not very romantic. Do you ride around visiting people all the time?"

Dwight watched his horse coming toward him. The boy was digging his heels in its ribs, but it held to its steady plod. "Nope. Six days of the week I'm a shoe salesman."

"Sell shoes! That's sure not romantic. Being a sea captain or something—that would be. Do you make lots of money?"

"Matter of fact I do. I have in mind to earn myself a hundred thousand dollars, and I got over five thousand dollars in the bank already."

"Oh." She looked at him with big wide eyes. "Maybe being a shoe salesman isn't so bad."

His paint pony slogged to a stop in front of him. The boy slid to the ground a lot easier than he had climbed up.

"See you at Sunday school!" Dwight took his horse's reins and swung aboard.

"Say, 'Thank you,' Robert," snapped the little girl sternly. "That man has a lovely lady friend and a fine job. Mind your manners."

The boy muttered something and then grumbled something else with "Sis" in it to the girl.

With a cheerful wave, Dwight was on his way again. He smiled to himself. Yes, he had a lovely lady and a fine job. They were not by his own doing, of course; they were both the gifts and workings of his Lord.

Best of all, he was making his fortune as a salesman in the city he liked best in the whole world. He couldn't be happier!

12

More Important Than Shoes

Two seagulls, one white and one not-so-white, dipped and soared in the clean blue sky. They sailed away beyond the rooftops. Lovely day!

With a broom, Dwight chased a little cloud of dust out the shoe store door. So he was working in a shoe store again—no more traveling, for Mr. Henderson had died, and his business dissolved. At least Dwight had a good job again.

Dwight recognized the customer coming into the store. It was one of the teachers from the Sunday school, Mr. Hibbert.

Dwight greeted him with a cheerful grin. "Mr. Hibbert, good morning, sir. What can I sell you today?"

"Sell? Nothing today, D. L." He smiled weakly.

"Then what else can I do for you?"

"Recently, when I was ill, you took my Sunday school class."

"Those girls!" Dwight snorted. "They laughed in my face. I came very near kicking the lot of them out. Didn't, of course."

"Those girls. Yes. Well, I am still most ill. My doctor says I will die if I remain in this climate. My lungs. Consumption. I must go home to New York state." His coughing sounded terrible.

What do you say to a man whose lungs seem to be ripping loose? "What can I do, Mr. Hibbert?"

"I have never led any of my class to Christ. I think I've hurt them more than helped them."

Dwight was all ready to say something to make Mr. Hibbert feel good. But he didn't. He had never thought about that before. Always he fretted when he brought less than a thousand children into his Sunday school. Twelve or fifteen hundred children pleased him better. Numbers. Huge numbers. And yet, why? Which was more important: to drag in the numbers or to show them the Jesus whom Dwight served?

"I would suppose you want to tell them how you feel."

"But not at Sunday school, D. L. In their homes. I want to visit each girl personally.

More Important Than Shoes

I'm too weak to drive a carriage—"

"I'll handle that, if you want to go."

Where had Dwight himself met Jesus? Not at Sunday school, though he learned something about Christ there. He had met Jesus in the back room of his uncle's store, with shoe boxes and the smell of new leather all about. His own Sunday school teacher had taken Jesus out of the church (where one expects Jesus to be) and put Him where Dwight was every day.

Now here was Dwight's chance to do the same. He did not look forward to all those visits. Ride all over Chicago's poor district with a dying man? Not very cheerful. But he had said he would, and Dwight Moody's word was good.

It took them ten days. They climbed rickety stairs to shabby little apartments. They talked and prayed. Mr. Hibbert showed his girls that, without Jesus, dying is only dying; that Jesus alone gives the soul wings. Each girl. Every girl in his class.

On the evening of the eleventh day, Dwight rode down to the train station for a very sad farewell. He knew Mr. Hibbert was going home to die.

Mr. Hibbert sat quietly on a cast iron bench beside the train car as a porter loaded his baggage. Impatient, the sweaty engine blasted a cloud of steam into the dank night air.

Dwight smiled. "That meeting last night at your house. What a blessing! Even if we didn't quite get through the song." He remembered the words to "Blest Be the Tie That Binds" now. He sure couldn't remember them last night.

"Every single girl saved." Mr. Hibbert beamed. "What joy!"

"I would rather die than lose that blessing I got last night. And now I thought I might see you off."

"You're not alone." Mr. Hibbert nodded beyond Dwight.

Here came Peggy, one of the girls from class. She walked slowly along the train platform. She seemed not quite sure she should be here. From over there came two more girls.

Now the platform churned with lively girls all clustered around Mr. Hibbert. A few days ago they had been lost, without purpose or eternal life. Tonight every one was pledged to Jesus.

"All A-boooarrrd!" the conductor yelled.

Mary with the lovely soprano voice tried again to get "Blest Be the Tie That Binds" started. Dwight remembered the words all right, but he couldn't sing them. Neither could the others. The song fell apart amid tears and sobs.

The train lurched forward. Mr. Hibbert stepped aboard on the rearmost car. The black engine dissolved in the darkness somewhere up ahead. The unseen smokestack spit crackling yellow and orange sparks. The whistle hooted.

Mr. Hibbert stood on the platform of the back car, one hand and finger pointing to heaven. Heaven! Yes! They would all meet there! The blackness swallowed Mr. Hibbert, train, and all.

What had happened these last two weeks? Dwight thought about Mr. Hibbert's devotion. He thought about the joy of watching these girls come to Jesus one by one. He had never felt such joy selling shoes!

Money? A hundred thousand dollars? Piffle. Money was not important. Jesus was. Telling about Jesus—selling Jesus; that was the thing! Dwight L. Moody, super salesman, suddenly had something more important to sell than shoes.

13

Emma

Dwight knocked at the door nervously. What would Emma say? He liked Emma. In fact he liked her very much. In fact—

He liked her so much he hated to displease her. Especially, he did not want to make her quit liking him back. But this crazy notion of his just might do it.

The huge carved oak door of the Revell house opened by inches. And there she stood in the narrow gap by the doorjamb, smiling, and Dwight's heart sang like a canary. She was just so pretty.

She invited him in most politely, and he followed her to the ornate parlor. The Revells were prominent people in Chicago; their house reflected their importance. Emma's wealthy parents didn't think too much of this country boy with the rough speech. But at least they didn't chase Dwight off when he came calling.

She invited him to sit. He sat. She offered tea. He declined. He was too nervous; he might dribble it on the rug accidentally or something.

"Emma, last week I went out with Mr. Hibbert, one of the teachers at our Sunday school. We visited every girl in his class, and every girl ended up committing herself to Jesus. It was the greatest, most glorious blessing I've ever had."

She smiled brightly. "I'm so happy, D. L.! That must have been wonderful!"

"It was! It was. So wonderful—" Dwight stopped for a big, deep, from-the-bottom breath. And another "—that I've quit my job of selling shoes."

She looked at him blankly. "What about that hundred thousand dollars you're going to earn?"

"All of a sudden it ain't important. I've got a taste of another world, Emma, and I don't care no more for making money."

"Where will you live? It takes money to live; pay your room and board at the boarding house. Clothes. You even have to buy your own shoes retail if you quit selling them. All that."

"The YMCA rents a little room in a church

where I can stay for free in return for holding meetings. And I can—"

"In a church? It doesn't even have a kitchen, does it?"

"Don't need a kitchen. Emma, I'll be doing missionary work right in the heart of the worst part of the city. It's a dream I've had a long time."

"Or any proper furniture."

"That don't matter."

"D. L., it's crazy. The whole notion's crazy. You'll starve to death if the rats don't eat you first. You can't—"

"There's restaurants to eat in, and the room's got benches to sleep on and—"

"Did you see that picture the newspaper made? You on your old horse, riding around town?"

"Inviting children to Sunday school. Yep."

"And the paper was suggesting maybe you were a little crazy then. Do you realize what they'll say about you now—if you give up your job and income for this fool idea?"

"I've thought this over long and hard, Emma. I'm sure if I devote myself to God's business, God will take care of me. I want to sell Jesus just the way I sold shoes."

"D. L., that's even crazier! Religion is not shoes!"

"But I am me. I'm a salesman. It's my

strong point, the thing I do best. I figure God will take my strong point and use it for His work. Don't you see?"

Her beautiful face was pinched together in a sorry frown. No, she did not see; he could tell. But she was young, only fifteen. She just didn't understand how important this was.

When Dwight left the lavish Revell home a while later, he still had not convinced her. But she had not changed his mind, either.

He was young, and he was enthusiastic, and he was one cracker-jack salesman. God could really use him. God *would* use him! He could not go mooning around about Emma Revell, pretty as she was. He must get ready to speak tonight at the services they were holding at North Market Hall. And he must get his YMCA meetings planned out.

This being a missionary to the slums full time was an adventure—exciting!—and he looked forward to tackling the rough customers from the north end docks and bars.

Now if he could just get Emma to see the excitement—

14

The War

When the winter wind comes screaming off the lake at you, you might just as well curl into a little ball in front of the woodstove and go to sleep. The lake front is bitter misery then. But when a warm spring breeze wanders up from the farmlands south of town—what a joy!

Dwight strolled along the lakeshore. To his right, the water flapped quietly against the stone wall separating lake from land. A soft breeze pushed at him from behind and mussed his hair. He thought of spring back home on the farm—the mud, the wet air, and the cheerful birds.

The portly man on Dwight's left tugged at his collar. "April. Love April."

"The best month," Dwight agreed, "usually. When nobody's using April to start a war with."

"That business at Fort Sumter? Couple Southern hotheads. That'll be over with in a few months. States can't just leave the Union whenever they feel like it. Lincoln will straighten it out."

Dwight nodded. "Lincoln's a farm boy—like me. But he speaks well; lots better'n me. And smart, too. If anyone can save the day, he can."

The chubby man laughed. "Don't put me on, boy! Talking like you know him face to face."

"I do. He was passing through Chicago on one of his campaign trips. He heard about my Sunday school and come to visit it one Sunday. Not a voter in the building, either, 'cept the teachers. He told my classes, 'You're all in the right place and learning the right things.' God-fearing man, Mr. Lincoln."

Dwight grinned, remembering another time. "And then there was the joke I thought I pulled on that farmer."

"What farmer?"

Dwight stopped beside the lapping water. "I was on a train down at the south end of the state. Train had stopped at a small town, and I was in the train car, leaning on the open window, looking out.

"Along comes this quiet farmer sort; just a plain man. Thought I might have some fun with him. So I said, 'Say! Do you know that Lincoln's on this train?'

"His eyes get big, and his ears prick up. 'No! Is he?' asks he.

"And I says, 'Don't think he is. I was just asking if *you* knew that he was.'"

The portly man wagged his head and chuckled politely.

"But then, a little while later, here he comes walking back; same farmer. And he says, 'Our town's had some excitement, you know.'

"And I says, 'What's the matter?'

"And he says 'The authorities wouldn't let some folks bury a woman.'

"'Why not?' I asked.

"'She wasn't dead,' he says."

The whole front half of the portly gentleman bobbed up and down with laughter. "Guess he got you good!"

"Don't I guess! What's this?" Dwight walked over to a little newsstand. He picked up a newspaper. It was so fresh off the press you could smell the ink. The newsboy held out his hand. Dwight had to fish a minute to find the right change.

The portly man looked over Dwight's shoulder. "So Lincoln is blockading the Southern ports. That ought to choke them off."

"And on the fifteenth, it says here, he called

for troops. I don't know what to do. I should enlist. You know that. I've been a staunch believer in abolition for years—used to go to meetings in Boston." The luckless slave Anthony Burns forced himself into Dwight's memory. Dwight went on. "Now here the problem is coming to a head, and I ought to be supporting it."

"You have an important work here, though. You teach Sunday school every week and preach in two places Sunday mornings and evenings. And there's the Sunday school conventions. And the YMCA meetings."

Dwight nodded and ambled on along the waterfront. "And the prayer meetings. In the last six months I've only been home a couple evenings. Meetings all the rest of the time."

"You're obviously doing God's work."

"But I owe my country allegiance, too. President Lincoln sent out that call for recruits. The Bible says the powers that be are ordained of God. That's President Lincoln."

"The Bible also says thou shalt not kill."

"I thought of that, too." Dwight stopped and let the breeze ruffle his hair. "You're a member of the YMCA board. You respect God's will. What should I do?"

"Pray about it?"

"Course I did. I still don't know what to do."

The portly man smiled. The breeze didn't

seem to ruffle him at all. "The board already discussed it. Camp Douglas is just a short way south of town. The YMCA can pay your support as a chaplain to the soldiers. You travel down to the camp for service and such as they need and handle as many of your chores in town here as you can manage."

"Do both!" Dwight's heart made a happy little jump. "Great!"

"Now if this fiendish skirmish lasts more than a couple months, we'll see about sending you farther afield. Up to the front and the fighting. Maybe build you a temporary chapel. Whatever."

Dwight's heart sang like a meadowlark on a fence post! He could serve God *and* the YMCA *and* his country *and* President Lincoln *and* the people in his Sunday services! Of course the fighting wouldn't last long. Everyone agreed that this tiff between the Northern states and the Southern states would be ended shortly. Surely, hardly any people would actually die.

But they did, more than 529,000.

And the war lasted four long years.

15

Schoolhouse Hospital

It used to be a schoolhouse, but it wasn't anymore. Now it was a field hospital. The benches and desks were all stacked outside, getting rained on. Once upon a time, in the school yard, children laughed and played tag. Today bleeding men lay under thin woolen blankets in the rain and moaned for water.

It was lunch hour. Not long ago the inside would have smelled of children's apples and homemade gingerbread. Instead it smelled like dead rats; that's how bad infections smell. War does terrible things to men, and to schoolhouses, and to children.

Dwight stood in the school yard a few moments as the rain soaked through to his shoulders. He did not much feel like going inside. He watched the rain dimple a thin, glassy puddle by the schoolhouse door.

The front door flew open. A gray little man

came breezing out. His shirt had once been white, but careless laundering had grayed it. His pants used to be dark blue, probably, but too much sun had bleached them gray. A hayfield of unmown gray whiskers framed his mouth, and a thick bush of gray hair tangled around his ears.

He stopped to stare at Dwight a moment. "You the chaplain?"

"D. L. Moody. You're in charge of the hospital here?"

"Yep. Kinda young, ain't ya? No matter. The soldiers is younger. Kids. Kids is all they are. This-a-way." His head bobbed once, toward the door.

Dwight followed. Smells of rot and death came pouring out the door as he stepped through it. The schoolhouse consisted of one big classroom and a smaller cloak room off to the side. The cloak room had been turned into the surgery. Dwight could just see the end of a blood-stained table in its doorway.

Here in the main room men lay on row upon row of straw-stuffed burlap pads—misery multiplied by the score. Dwight could hardly walk around for stepping on someone.

The gray old man waded through the suffering. He pointed. "Young feller in that corner. Talk to him first. Yep, that one. Soon's you're done I got another'n over here."

Dwight expected to see a man in pain, and full of sorrow. No doubt the young man hurt terribly, but he was smiling.

"D. L. Moody. Chaplain, associated with the YMCA out of Chicago." Dwight sat down beside the young man's rough and lumpy little mattress. He extended his right hand to shake.

Still grinning the young man extended his left; his right arm was gone. "Private Harry Darke, sir. Howdy do."

"Howdy do, Harry. What's your outfit?"

"C. F. Smith's division, sir." The young man beamed.

"Call me D. L. Ever'one else does. I hear you did a fine job of bottling up the enemy."

"Yessir! I mean, D. L. The Confederates were just about to fight their way out and escape when we came charging up on 'em. Stopped 'em cold, and the whole caboodle surrendered. Captured ourselves fifteen thousand rebel soldiers. The whole of Fort Donelson. You hear about General Grant's terms? What he told the Confederate fort commander?"

"I guess I did! The whole North has by now. 'No terms except an immediate and unconditional surrender will be accepted.' Same as God's terms, exactly." Dwight was doing now what he loved to do best. He was talking about Jesus one-on-one with a man who did not yet know Him.

"God's terms?" The grin turned upside down to become a puzzled frown.

"Sure! God wants you to give yourself up to Him, lock, stock and barrel. He wants you to admit you're a sinner. Everybody is, y'know. He knows you are, too, but He wants you to tell Him so anyway. He wants you to say out loud that you understand how Jesus died to pay for all your sins. Shed His blood."

Private Darke turned suddenly grim. "Guess I know what shed blood looks like. I sure saw enough of it these two days of battle. Men falling all around me—my own blood—"

"The blood of Jesus was pure, and it paid off every sin debt. You agree to that. Then you swear you're going to live for Him from now on. Promise to live life His way. That's what God wants with unconditional surrender. And now, too."

"I'll think about that. Thankee, D. L."

"*Immediate* surrender, Harry. That means right now. Not tomorrow. You might up and die before tomorrow. You'd be lost."

"Well, uh—until I understand better—"

"Won't do!" Dwight studied the frayed edges of his Bible. His poor Bible was taking a beating out here. "You see, Harry, God likes to start at the beginning. When I accepted Je-

Schoolhouse Hospital 83

sus I didn't know beans about Him. But I determined to be His man. And I've never regretted that. Since then He's been teaching me what He wants me to know. He'll teach you."

"Yes, but—"

"So until you become His, the way I just explained, He can't start working on you. He can't give you eternal life. He can't teach you wonderful things about Himself, and He can't bless you the way He wants to."

"He's blessed you, huh? And taught you?"

Dwight bobbed his head. "For instance. I thought that the more numbers I got into my Sunday school classes, the better I was doing. Then He showed me that it wasn't just numbers. It's what you do for those children —whether you lead them to Jesus."

The young man's eyes looked glassy, and tiny beads of sweat had popped out on his forehead.

Dwight kept talking fast. "He taught me that you can't wait with this stuff. Sometimes I'd be talking to fellers one day and the next day, poof. They're gone. Dead in battle, or dead of disease. And lost."

"I don't expect to die just yet. I'll survive this."

"Sure you will! And you can't spend the rest of your life any better than to let God bless you. And to work for Him."

"Reckon He'd do that for me?"

"Now you listen, Harry!" Dwight wagged a finger in his face. "You accept Jesus because He wants you to and not because He might do something for you if you do. See what I mean? Unconditional surrender. Even if He does nothing for you at all."

"I see." The young man met Dwight's eye squarely, thoughtfully. "Not what He does for me. What He does with me."

"That's it entirely!" Dwight felt good. He felt wonderful! He didn't mind the ugly stench in this sorry schoolhouse. He didn't mind the discomfort of traveling through the February rain all the way to Tennessee here. He didn't mind the problems of preaching evening services to wounded soldiers like these, even as nearby guns and mortars were creating new wounded while he spoke.

He almost didn't mind leaving Emma Revell behind in Chicago. Almost. He was afraid this war would drag on for years; she feared it would last forever. She talked about getting married. She was right. They shouldn't wait for the war to end.

But Emma was in Chicago, and Dwight was here outside Fort Donelson in Tennessee. And beside him lay a young man in prayer, giving himself to Jesus. The boy was no older

Schoolhouse Hospital

than Dwight had been when Dwight accepted Jesus. What would God please to do with this proud young man with only one arm?

Late that night, in the cold, heavy darkness and the thunderous silence that follows battle, God pleased to take that one-armed young man up to heaven.

16

God's Man

They were called hedgerows over here—waist-high fences made out of living shrubbery. They draped like green garlands across these gentle English hills, dividing the velvet meadows into square upon square.

"Ah! Now what is that?" Dwight pointed as a plump little bird squirted up out of the hedgerow and flew back into it a hundred feet on ahead.

"Robin redbreast. I hear you have a robin redbreast in America." The Reverend Henry Varley's thick English accent made his speech difficult to understand. He spoke earnestly, intently, even when he was only talking about British birds.

"We do." Dwight continued along the quiet little English lane. "But it doesn't look quite the same. Ours is not so plump, and it has a larger bill."

"Much of what is here in England and over there in your America is similar but not quite the same. Don't you think?"

"Absolutely. And I am enjoying this visit! Enjoying the differences."

The Reverend Varley paused to wave his walking stick in the air. "Buzzard up there; I think you Americans call them hawks."

High in the powder-gray sky, a hawk set its stubby wings and coasted in a wide, sweeping circle.

Dwight thought of the marsh hawks in his Connecticut Valley so long ago. How he had yearned to leave there—to find freedom! Now here he was, across the Atlantic Ocean. But his freedom came from loving God, not from traveling somewhere.

"Your civil war has been over two years now, hasn't it?" the Englishman asked.

"April of 1865. Yes. Two years, almost exactly. Such a sad, sad business. The North is just now picking up the pieces, and the South will be many years recovering. Many years."

The Englishman wagged his head. "England's had her share of civil war. I understand." Then he brightened. "Have you found what you came to England to find?"

"I have! We both have." Dwight watched the soaring hawk a moment longer. "I married my Emma in 1862, a year after the war began, while I was a chaplain."

"Loveliest bride in America, no doubt!"

"I guess so! When baby Emma came along I was all wrapped up in the Chicago YMCA. We built a fine new hall—biggest in town—and gathered in a lot of money for work among the poor. And all the while I was preaching at one church and teaching Sunday school in another."

"Busy days."

"Productive. But busy. Then I realized that Emma was not well. She had this persistent cough. Asthma, the doctor said. He suggested sea air might help."

"So you took an ocean voyage to England. Why England?"

Dwight grinned, and fifteen years melted away; he felt like a fifteen-year-old again. "Dream-chasing. I've always been a dream chaser. I've long dreamed of hearing Charles Spurgeon preach. Meeting George Müller's been another dream."

"And you did?"

"I did." Dwight stopped. "When Dr. Spurgeon spoke it seemed as though he spoke directly to me, though I was in the balcony. I felt—" Dwight waved a hand, trying to pluck the right word from the dank air; he couldn't grasp it. "I felt that God was telling me something, but I couldn't quite hear what."

The graying old Englishman grunted and walked on. He poked at the dirt in the quiet lane with his walking stick. "Spurgeon and Müller are eloquent servants of God. Fine men through whom our Lord can speak to you."

"But He spoke through you. Last night in your prayer meeting."

The Reverend Varley's eyes burned into Dwight's. "Indeed! And what did He say?"

" 'The world has yet to see what God can do with one man wholly committed to Him.' "

"I remember saying that, yes. But I didn't know—"

"I want to be that man! Ever since I first said yes to Jesus, it's been 'What can D. L. the salesman do for God?' From now on, it's 'What can God do with plain D. L.?' Don't you see?"

The Englishman smiled; it was the first smile Dwight had ever seen on the man. "God bless you, D. L.! God bless you and use you!"

That hawk was still around, little more than a sweeping, circling dot way up high. It climbed unseen air currents and drifted chained to unseen winds. Even the soaring hawk could not taste real freedom, for it could fly only where the breezes and the seasons allowed it to.

Thanks to God's patience, Dwight was no longer chained to anything—not even to things unseen. D. L. Moody, ex-salesman, at last was truly free!

17

The Big Fire

The huge double doors of the firehouse swung open just in time; two massive Percheron horses came bursting out into the street. The bells on their collars jangled. A big brass bell clanged on the fire engine they were pulling. Dogs started barking all up and down the street.

Clattering, lumbering, snorting, the great horses galloped south down Ashland. The bright red fire engine with its shiny brass fittings glittered in the evening light.

Somewhere to the south, still another fire siren wailed.

A ragged boy stood up on his tenement steps. "Must be one grand fire somewheres near! Look at the smoke!"

A broad gray curtain, dark at the bottom and nearly white at the top, covered the clear autumn sky downtown.

The boy looked right up into Dwight's face. "Mr. Moody? Do you suppose the whole city will burn up?"

Dwight grinned. "Now you saw that there big fire engine go clanging by just now. Chicago's got the best fire equipment made! Best firemen, too. Fires ain't no match for our fire department."

"Yeah!" The boy laughed. He ran down the street to climb a lamp post for a better look.

Dwight watched the thick smoke grimly. "South of the river?"

Beside him, Ira Sankey looked worried. "Appears so. The fire better stay there, too. The waterworks are up here; if the water system goes, the whole city burns."

"Lucky we have Lake Michigan to draft out of." Dwight rubbed his hands together. "Let's get going; lots to do yet tonight."

Mr. Sankey nodded. Dwight noticed that even as he walked, Mr. Sankey kept one eye on the smoke.

The day felt strange—on edge. Dwight could not see why that should be. This Sunday was like any other. There had been nothing out of the ordinary at the Illinois Street Church that morning. Dwight had preached there just as usual.

After lunch—that's when it started. When Dwight tutored his class of Sunday school

The Big Fire 93

teachers, they seemed nervous. Maybe it was the dry, crackly wind; weather often affects you that way. August had been dry, and September even drier. Now, on October 8, there was hot wind and still no rain. Another fire bell clanged somewhere.

Here they were at Farwell Hall for evening service. Dwight would preach, as he usually did. Mr. Sankey would sing; what a glorious singer was Mr. Sankey! This day felt out of joint, but the worship service would surely end it well.

Not so. People squirmed. Mr. Sankey sounded nervous even when he sang. Dwight's sermon did not go well at all. Out in the streets men were shouting. Fire equipment rumbled by; hooves clattered; bells clanged. Dogs were barking all over town.

Usually, Dwight never closed a sermon without an invitation to unsaved listeners to come forward, committing themselves to Jesus. This Sunday evening he gave no such call. His sermon fizzled to a close. The hall emptied quickly.

Dwight headed for the door. He stepped out into the street and stopped. He gaped, shocked.

He could hear the fire howl and crackle south of the river. You could smell the smoke —and see it, too! It boiled up, filling the southern sky. It glowed red-orange near the ground. Higher up, it churned black and ugly. Here and there a wild burst of white fire would splash up through the thick pall.

"Looks like half of Chicago!" Dwight whispered.

"We'd better hurry home, D. L." Ira Sankey's warm tenor voice creaked with fear. "My Fanny will worry."

"Yes." Dwight started north, almost at a run. Emma would worry, too. *Dwight* was worried!

He had met Ira Sankey less than a year ago. He had insisted Mr. Sankey move from Pennsylvania to join him in the ministry. Now here was Mr. Sankey in Chicago in a brand new house because D. L. Moody asked him to come.

Dwight and Emma and the children lived in a bright new house, too. Members of the church had given it to them as a surprise. And then there were Farwell Hall and the Illinois Street Church. Dwight had been God's instrument in building both. Surely God would not wipe all that out. Surely the fire would stay on the south side of the river.

Crowds of refugees poured north along the main streets. Some rode in carriages. Most walked. A few pushed wheelbarrows or drove horse-drawn carts. Every cart and wagon

The Big Fire

was full to overflowing with children and trunks and odd bits of furniture.

Their faces! Dwight's heart ached. They were losing everything they could not carry up these dull orange streets.

He paused on the front steps of his new home to gaze once more upon disaster. Earth and sky roared, ablaze together, from one side of the town to the other, as far as he could see.

This wild inferno would take half the city before it was put out. Homes and shops, railroad yards and factories, churches and schools would be all gone! Only the river would stop it.

Tomorrow, Monday morning, Dwight must organize his church members. There would be much work to do for the unfortunate fire victims on the South Side. At 11:00, he and his family finally got to bed.

At midnight they were up again. The fire had jumped the river! As Dwight's family fled town with all the other refugees, flames reached the waterworks. The city's fire hydrants went dry.

The howling red blaze had won the fight. It ate its way through block after block, and no one could stop it. It ate Farwell Hall, the Illinois Street Church, the mission, all the tenements Dwight's Sunday school students lived in, Dwight's own new house, and Ira Sankey's. Everything built of wood dissolved to ashes. The city he loved so much shriveled to stinking, black rubble.

More than 300 people died in that fire. Some had been at Dwight's evening service.

Dwight Moody, shoe salesman, preacher and evangelist, would do many wonderful things for God, and God would do even more wonderful things through him. But his whole life long, D. L. Moody would always regret that on that one horrible night of nights he had failed to call his hearers to Jesus Christ.

18

Mr. Moody's School

The ancient Greeks told an old story about a beautiful bird called the phoenix. Only one ever existed at any one time, the Greeks said. At the end of 500 years, that one bird would build a great fire and burn itself up.

From the ashes would rise a brand new phoenix, just as gorgeous, in gold and iridescent purple. The new phoenix would live five hundred years, then repeat the cycle. Well, that's what the Greeks said.

"A phoenix. Chicago is a phoenix." Dwight rode down LaSalle Street in a light carriage. "Ashes in seventy-one. That was fourteen years ago. Now look at her!"

The carriage wheels echoed between hard, strong buildings on either side. Wagons and carriages choked the street. People hurried about; dogs barked. The city was whole again.

A wiry little woman, Emma Dryer, sat beside him in the carriage. "Yes! And very few wooden buildings, you'll notice. Almost all stone and brick. She's far less likely to immolate herself again. Burn herself up, I mean."

Dwight nodded. "Not exactly fireproof, but almost. And such splendid new buildings." He spied a shabby-looking warehouse.

"Except for a few."

"Driver, stop," Emma ordered. The carriage creaked to a halt. "Now that very warehouse, brother Moody, is one of our places. Cheap rent. We hold classes downstairs, and the upstairs is a sizeable dormitory."

"The building's a dump. Jesus Christ and His gospel deserve first-rate facilities. If big business can go in style, so should Christians. No better cause—or business—than the cause of Jesus."

She sat primly in the carriage seat, slim as wire cable and twice as strong. She twisted to look at him. "Ten years ago I traveled clear to New York to enlist your help. Chicago here needed a Bible school for lay people. A school with dormitory space because so many students would live too far off to travel daily to classes."

"And I said no. I still say no. Not practical," said Dwight.

"It's working, in a way. The students stay

Mr. Moody's School

in the dorms while they attend classes. But we're not organized. We rent buildings like this all over town, but we're not truly together. We still need you and your business skills, brother Moody. We need you to put your weight and reputation behind this."

"For what? Sounds like you're doing well."

"To gather these scattered little knots of people all over the city and organize them."

"Organize them into what?"

She fluttered her hand, frustrated. "A—a school. You know—a real school to train men and women as lay workers. Driver—on!"

The carriage lurched forward.

Dwight sighed and sat back. "My business skills, eh? All right. As a businessman I'm sure that loans and debts are never a good way. Cash in hand. Build your financial backlog, and then I'll talk school with you."

"How much?"

"Quarter million. Two-hundred-fifty thousand and not a penny less—not to do it right. And I won't do it any other way."

"You'll be back next January?"

"Yes. Four months of preaching. Evangelizing."

"I'll talk to you then." Her firm little mouth tightened. "With the money, Lord willing."

Lord willing. How often people said that

but didn't really mean it. Dwight knew that Emma Dryer meant it. She was a teacher, very well educated. Why, she could be the dean of any school in the country, just about. Yet she devoted her life to teaching Bible classes to common men and women—the men and women God so preferred to use. That was determination, and only determination could raise such a huge sum of money.

But raise it she did. Within a year, Dwight prowled the streets of the city he loved, pointing out this building or that. "Buy this. Tear down that and rebuild."

The Bible students followed his advice and accepted his leading. Those scattered little bunches of sheep came together into a good, solid flock. They became the Chicago Evangelization Society—and eventually the Moody Bible Institute.

Dwight didn't get to Chicago often. He traveled all over the country holding evangelistic meetings. He spent the summers in Northfield where he had started other schools and conferences. But constantly he got reports about the affairs of his school.

His school. Dwight Moody's school.

The farm boy who never finished school himself had brought together an institute for the Lord's work.

19

Going Home

Dwight Lyman Moody, shoe salesman turned free-lance evangelist, was bushed. No wonder. He would be sixty-three years old in a couple of months—no young colt anymore. And here he was gallivanting all over the country.

Maybe he should heed his doctors' advice and take things a little easier. He leaned back in his bunk and listened awhile to the familiar clickety-clickety-clickety of the railroad car. Railroads sure made travel easy!

A young man named Hank pulled open the curtain beside Dwight's ear. "Anything I can do for you, D. L.?"

"Nope; thanks. Doing fine."

The young man smiled. The curtain dropped back into place.

Dwight remembered the uncomfortable benches on the old-style railroad cars. This fancy Pullman car was such a great improvement. By day it had seats like any other car. By night, the seats folded into beds—the lower berth. Still more beds—the upper berth—came folding out from the wall above. Curtains made each berth into a sort of private little room.

When you felt so tired, as Dwight did now, the lower berth bed was a mighty comfortable place to rest, day or night.

The clickety-clicks slowed. Dwight watched the country flow by outside the window. November is too cold a month to be opening windows; even so he could hear the huff-puff of the locomotive. Now and then a cloud of sooty smoke from the steam engine drifted by—another reason not to open windows!

Dwight tapped on the curtain.

The young man opened it. "Yes, D. L.?"

"We're coming into Detroit now, I take it."

Hank nodded. "And an hour late, too. If we don't make up at least half an hour on the run to Niagara, we're going to miss our connection to Boston and home."

"God'll run the show the way He wants it. He always has."

"Yes, sir! But I can't resist prodding Him a little." Hank grinned. He disappeared, and the curtain fell back into place.

Going Home

Shimmying and rattling, the train dragged itself to a casual stop in Detroit's huge railroad station. The locomotive sighed a thick white cloud of steam. Its bell clanged.

Passengers scrambled off and on; baggage piled up here as piles of baggage disappeared over there. People shouted. The busyness in a railroad depot was like ants around an ant hill—go, go, go.

There stood Hank on the platform, talking earnestly to a chubby fellow in gray-striped overalls. Probably the engineer. It must be great fun to run a train.

Dwight thought of the sad wail of train whistles back when he was a boy in Northfield. They made him feel restless then and eager to travel. Now they called him home—to Northfield.

The Great Fire of Chicago was a distant memory now. That had been eighteen years ago. Since then so much had happened. Dwight had preached and Ira Sankey had sung to many thousands of people. They had been hardly known when they held meetings overseas in Ireland, Scotland, and England. No one was more surprised than they when they returned to America and found out they were famous evangelists.

They drew huge crowds in Brooklyn, in Philadelphia—everywhere they went, it seemed.

They even drew crowds at the Chicago World's Fair six years ago. Chicago, once a blackened ruin, was a magnificent city again, all recovered from its horror.

Dwight, who had never finished school himself, was God's instrument for building schools. He had started schools and seminaries here in Northfield. He had helped the Bible Institute in Chicago get going. The Institute trained hundreds of workers for the ministry. God's work would go on. Chicago. Dear old Chicago.

Chicago had been made new. Dwight had been made new, even if his aching body now felt pretty old. He remembered when he was fifteen—how he froze up if he had to speak in public. Wasn't that a long time ago? He had spoken to hundreds of thousands since then.

Dwight had spent much of his life traveling about on the Lord's business. Now he was coming home to rest. The weariness weighed heavily on his chest now, as if someone large were sitting on him.

The engineer walked away toward the locomotive, and Hank came back aboard. Moments later, the railroad car shuddered and began to move. The train whistle hooted.

Hank stuck his head in through the curtain, grinning like a little boy with a brand new lollipop. "I just talked to the engineer. I mentioned you were on board. He says he was converted fifteen years ago because of your preaching, and he's been a happy man ever since. Told me to tell you one of your friends is at the throttle—and to hold your breath. We'll make it."

Make it they did. When Dwight awakened next morning, his car was coupled to the Boston train. He was coming home.

Home. Good old Chicago was home. Northfield certainly was home. Dwight had felt curiously at home in the Holy Land on a two-month visit there seven years ago. He traveled so much that even this railroad car felt a little like home.

And yet none of those places was home, really. When this overweight, under-strong body of his finally gave out—that's when he'd be going home, home to Jesus. "D. L.'s coronation day" he called it.

The familiar Massachusetts countryside rumbled by his train window. Emma knew he was coming; he had sent a telegram ahead. He regretted cutting the Kansas City campaign short, even if it was because of his illness.

He stuffed the regret into the back of his mind. That was God's concern, not his. This was not D. L. doing something *for* God; it was God doing something *with* D. L. What did

God have in mind next for D. L. Moody?

That November in 1899 neither the former shoe salesman nor those who knew him realized just what God had in mind. Dwight's heart, overworked for years, began to fail.

He made it up the stairs when he got home, but he did not walk down again. On December 22, surrounded by the people he loved, D. L. closed his eyes for the last time.

A half century before, a restless boy in Northfield listened to the trains and watched the hawks and yearned for freedom.

That young boy thought he was happy and free traveling. He thought he was even happier serving Jesus. He thought he was happiest when he let God work through him.

But on that coronation day three days before Christmas, ten days before a new century began, God showed His salesman what freedom and happiness really are.

The world has yet to see what God can do with one man wholly committed to Him.

When It Happened

1837 — February 5, Dwight Lyman Moody is born on his mother's birthday.

1841 — Edwin Moody, Dwight's father, dies; Dwight is four.

1854 — Restless to be free, Dwight travels to Boston and obtains work in his uncle's Holton Shoe Store. He becomes a top-rate shoe salesman. He *loves* selling!

1856 — Ed Kimball, Dwight's Sunday school teacher, leads him to Christ in the back room of the shoe store.

1856 — September. Still restless, Dwight travels west to Chicago, a loose, open, brawny city. He becomes a shoe salesman at Wiswell's Shoe Store. Soon he is eagerly involved in a slum mission Sunday school and other ministries.

1858 — Dwight and some other workers start their own Sunday school at North Market Street Hall.

1859 — He helps the dying Mr. Hibbert reach the girls in his Sunday school class. He sees that Jesus is important; making money isn't. Dwight quits his job (and regular income) to serve God full time. He becomes a leader in Chicago's YMCA (Young Men's Christian Association) as well as a preacher and a teacher.

1861 — The Civil War begins. Dwight serves as a chaplain, both near Chicago and on the battlefields. As soldiers die, he learns the importance of accepting Jesus Christ *now*.

1862 — Dwight marries Emma Revell. In a year and a little more, baby Emma is born.

1865 — The Civil War ends. Dwight's Sunday school classes are going well. He has built a church for the converts on the city's North Side, the Illinois Street Church. With his help and sales skills the YMCA builds Farwell Hall.

When It Happened

1867 — To help Emma's asthma, Dwight takes her traveling in England. There he hears the message that redirects his life: *The world has yet to see what God can do with one man wholly committed to Him.*

1869 — Baby Will is born. Dwight's congregation surprises him and his family with a new home of their own.

1870 — Dwight meets Ira Sankey at a Sunday school convention. What a marvelous singing voice! Moody and Sankey will become a world-famous partnership in the ministry.

1871 — October 8 and 9, Dwight's beloved city of Chicago burns. Gone are home and church and meeting hall. He has learned the hard way what is lasting and what is not.

1872 — June to September, Dwight travels again in England. He is invited to return for evangelistic meetings.

1873 — The Sankeys and Moodys go to England. In three years they reach thousands in Scotland, Ireland, and England. They return to America in August and find themselves world-famous evangelists.

1876 — Dwight lives awhile in Chicago. But he is free now—truly free in Jesus. No longer restless, he returns to Northfield, his hometown, to live. He spends summers there and October through April leading evangelistic meetings all over the United States. During the next five years he will establish schools, meetings, and conventions in the Northfield area.

1886 — With the help of Emma Dryer, Dwight encourages the Chicago Evangelistic Society to train Christian workers. The informal school at first holds classes in ratty buildings all over town. With Dwight's leadership, the Society becomes a centralized school with its own property and buildings. Eventually it will be called the Moody Bible Institute, a lasting monument to the farm boy from Massachusetts who became God's man.

1891 — Dwight and Ira Sankey go to Scotland for meetings.

1892 — On a preaching "vacation," they visit the Holy Land and Rome. Dwight's joy is to walk where Paul and Jesus walked.

1893 — Chicago hosts the World's Fair. The booming city is all rebuilt now. Dwight preaches to the fair visitors in any place big enough to handle the crowds. He even fills a huge circus tent each Sunday morning.

1899 — Dwight travels to California to preach. In November he leads meetings in Kansas City although he doesn't feel well. He returns to Northfield weak and ill.

1899 — December 22, on what he once called his coronation day, the troubled heart in his physical body fails. His soul's heart tastes a freedom beyond the wildest dreams of that restless little boy on the Northfield farm. D. L. goes to heaven.

Moody Press, a ministry of the Moody Bible Institute, is designed for education, evangelization, and edification. If we may assist you in knowing more about Christ and the Christian life, please write us without obligation: Moody Press, c/o MLM, Chicago, Illinois 60610.